Contents

Pathfinder 6

A CILT series for language teachers

Communication re-activated

Teaching pupils
with learning difficulties

Bernardette Holmes

Other titles in the PATHFINDER series:

  Recording progress (John Thorogood)
  Reading for pleasure in a foreign language (Ann Swarbrick)
  Schemes of work (Laurie Kershook)
  On target. Teaching in the target language (Susan Halliwell and Barry Jones)
  Yes - but will they behave? Managing the interactive classroom
    (Susan Halliwell)

Acknowledgements

I would like to thank the following colleagues for their support:

All the teachers involved in the development of the *Suffolk Graded Objectives in Modern Languages* - especially Steven Clarke for the wonderful weather pictures.

The teachers of Special Educational Needs and Foreign Languages included in the *Steps Towards Achievement Project*, Essex - especially Hazel Hibbard, Thurstable School, Tiptree for the brilliant wigwam card and Yvonne Bouteldja and Elaine Pryke for their inspirational efforts at St Benedict's Roman Catholic School, Colchester.

Erica Brown, Project Officer to *PALM* (Pupil Autonomy in Learning with Micro-electronics) for introducing me to the concept keyboard.

Jugendmagazin for first publishing 'Himmel und Hölle Spiel'.

This book is dedicated to my pupils for teaching me all I know about learning.

First published 1991
ISBN 0 948003 59 6

Cover by Logos Design & Advertising
Printed in Great Britain by Oakdale Printing Co Ltd

Published by Centre for Information on Language Teaching and Research, Regent's College, Inner Circle, Regent's Park, London NW1 4NS.

1   The challenge of languages for all

Dear Reader

Teaching modern languages across the ability range is always described as a challenge. Dealing with pupils with learning difficulties can even be seen as some kind of obstacle course or endurance test. So what is especially difficult about teaching languages to pupils with learning difficulties?

In putting together this *Pathfinder*, I would like to share some practical strategies and teaching methods, drawn from recent classroom experience, which have been well-received by the pupils and have produced positive results. Some of the 'recipes' may well seem familiar, based as they are on the 'good for you' ingredients of communicative teaching. However, the secret ingredient which turns the staple diet into the 'cordon bleu' is pupil involvement.

As we implement the National Curriculum for all learners, we will need to take a fresh approach towards our use of the target language, the way we deal with double lessons and manage resources. For some of us, pupils with learning difficulties may be an entirely new clientèle.

One of our chief concerns will be to cater for individual requirements. Some pupils will find reading a problem, whereas for others concentration and following aural instructions will prove tough-going. Some will learn more successfully in groups; others will prefer 'the quiet table in the corner', where they can work alone. In order to satisfy these needs we will have to offer a greater variety of activities. Different pupils will be doing different things at different times. Inevitably, this will place additional demands on resources and technical equipment, but much can be achieved by using our existing materials more flexibly and by allowing pupils a greater degree of freedom in choosing what they do. In this way, they can draw up their own 'menu for learning'.

So, where do we start? What presentation techniques will be effective? How can we support learners and develop their independence from the teacher? Is it feasible to use the target language for all classroom communication - bearing in mind that these pupils already have known learning difficulties? What sort of activities maintain their interest in languages over a five-year programme?

I hope that some of the techniques described in this *Pathfinder* will be helpful in providing some possible answers to these questions. There is no one method suitable for every teacher or every pupil. It is highly recommended to 'pick and mix'.

Bon appétit!

Bernadette Holmes

(Advisory teacher for modern foreign languages, Essex)

2   Active presentation

The place of visuals, mime, rhythm and song

Successful lessons rely on pupil response. Particularly where pupils have short concentration spans, we need to involve them actively in all phases of the lesson, including the presentation phase. Techniques which help them to remember new language and make it their own are invaluable. The more new language can be supported by visuals, mime, rhythmic chanting and song the better. All of these stimulate the memory and help to obviate the need for English.

Visuals

So what's new about using visuals?

From hieroglyphics to cave painting, the Highway Code to washing instructions, visuals have been an effective means of communication across the centuries.

But are we sure about that?
Does that circle with a cross through it mean that I can or cannot put the baby's romper suit in the tumble drier???

Visuals only work if everybody knows what they represent.

In the classroom we are using visuals to support new language and avoid the reliance on English. If we explain everything in English, it defeats the purpose. If the pupils cannot crack the code and work out what the visuals mean, they become confused and lose interest.

How can we overcome this problem?

Visuals alone are not enough. Visuals accompanied by mime and gesture go a long way towards offering a solution. They are especially effective when pupils supply the mimes from their own ideas. Some of my own pupils invented a name for this way of learning. They call the technique:

★   ACTION PICTURES

By inviting the pupils to think up their own 'action pictures', we are involving them right from the start in creating the lesson. We know that our visuals have been understood because the pupils have acted out what the new language means.
    Let us take a straightforward example from a self-contained topic like 'The weather'. To start with, all you need is an overhead projector, a set of visuals and thirty pupils, the livelier the better!

- The visuals are introduced, accompanied by funny mimes from the teacher.
- The pupils listen, repeat the language and imitate the mimes.
- Gradually, as the pupils gain in confidence, they can begin to supply their own 'action pictures' for the visuals.
- The class chooses the best 'action picture' for each visual, which they can then all copy.

Why does this work?

- Pupils can show that they understand by responding physically to what they hear and see.
- Everybody has something active to do from the outset - including the least able.
- Activity enlivens what is essentially an exercise in repetition.
- By thinking up and imitating the 'action pictures', pupils are designing their own support system for learning.
- A variety of games, combining mime and the use of visuals, can follow. In this way the new language can be thoroughly rehearsed before the pupils break into groups and begin to use the language more independently.

Rhythm

How can rhythm revive repetition?

Pupils with learning difficulties are likely to require more exposure and repetition of the language than more able learners. If we are not careful, repetition of the language, even accompanied by active response, can lead to unnaturally slow or mechanical production of the sounds. There needs to be plenty of variety of stimulus and pace.

Some of the simplest ideas for making the presentation of language more up-beat are usually the most effective, especially when they tap into the learners' own motivations. Here are some examples which show theory growing out of classroom practice, rather than the other way around.

★ RHYTHMIC CHANTING

Going into one 'difficult class', I was greeted by a young man with a decidedly set look, who alternated between clicking his fingers and moving his head sharply forward:

Click, click, headbutt, headbutt! Click, click, headbutt, headbutt!

Quite clearly, gaining his co-operation in the lesson was going to be vital, if anything positive was to be achieved - and this was only Monday period one! Armed with my trusty set of visuals for *Qu'est-ce qu'on va faire ce weekend?*, I made my way to the OHP and proceeded to introduce the language by clicking my fingers and chanting the new language items, line by line (see figure 1). The pupils joined in eagerly. 'Action pictures' soon developed to support each language item. With the pupils maintaining the pace by clicking their fingers between each phrase, activities could be selected at random from the transparency by using a pointer.

And what were the benefits?

- The fast pace provided *un peu de gymnastique de la mâchoire*, helping the pupils to get their mouths around the new sounds.
- Using the visuals to elicit the correct phrases and actions from the class showed that everybody understood what they were saying.
- Because everybody was having fun, nobody minded going over the same language items again and again.

Thanks to that young man, clicking fingers and rhythmic chanting has won a firm place in my repertoire of presentation techniques. Headbutts remain optional!

Figure 1   *Qu'est-ce qu'on va faire ce weekend?*

Légende

faire du vélo, jouer au foot, regarder la télé, écouter des disques, manger des bonbons, faire de la voile, jouer au golf, aller au ciné, prendre un pot, aller manger, faire du cheval, jouer aux cartes, aller à la disco, prendre des photos, aller nager, faire du ménage

★ THE FLASHCARD RAP

Flashcards will always be a reliable source of visual material and simple games like *Guess what's on the flashcard*, involving pupils in predicting which pictures are coming next, are popular favourites. However, before you can play the game, the language input still has to be made. This involves some form of presentation and repetition and no matter how attractive your flashcards are, it can sometimes be a bit of a struggle getting started!

Pupils with learning difficulties tend to need more stimulus to focus their attention and fix language in their memory. Using a rap rhythm can certainly invigorate proceedings and sustain their interest.

For example, taking a few brightly coloured flashcards of a disco, an ice-rink, a sports centre and so on, we can involve the pupils in the rhythm and movement of rap and turn repetition into an art form.

Je suis allé à la disco - disco, à la disco
Je suis allé à la patinoire - patinoire, à la patinoire
Je suis allé au centre de sports - centre de sports, au centre de sports!

This technique does not have to rely on the personality of the teacher. If you are not sure of your own capabilities when it comes to rap, all it takes is some collusion with the best rap artists in the class before the lesson begins. They will happily provide the rhythm and movement for you, enjoying being in the spotlight at the front of the class. Co-incidentally, these are usually the leaders of the pack, so by engaging their services we are promoting the positive image that learning foreign languages has street cred!

It is quite remarkable how rap helps pupils to recall language. It can be argued that they are only reciting chunks of pre-learnt language, but these 'pre-learnt chunks' form the building blocks of future communication. We can provide opportunities for pupils to move on from mere repetition to communication by using the same visual stimuli in information-gap tasks later on in the lesson.

For the more ambitious, sequences of pictures forming a short story can be introduced in this way and a real rap song can be created - and maybe recorded on tape!

Song

★ SETTING LANGUAGE TO POPULAR TUNES

Even with the best of presentation techniques, pupils with learning difficulties often forget what they have learnt from one lesson to the next. They need frequent opportunities to listen to and re-activate the language that is lying dormant in their memories. As we know, they also need variety, otherwise we fall foul of the *'done it all before'* syndrome. Song can help and the best tunes can come from unexpected sources.

At the time of the World Cup Summer 1990, I was asked to 'revisit' the topic of the weather with a disenchanted group of lower ability pupils in Year 9. Equipment was sparse, but we had managed to borrow an OHP. Clearly, funny mimes accompanying funny visuals ran the risk of sinking like a lead balloon and were not appropriate for this age-group. They had done the topic, but could not remember any of the necessary language. In some cases the pupils had genuine difficulty in recalling the phrases but others, who were a little more hostile, were merely reluctant to communicate. Fortunately, divine inspiration struck - the weather expressions fitted perfectly to the robust rendition of *Here we go!* and soon all of the learners were 'playing ball'. This is how it was done (see figure 2).

Figure 2   Song sheet for *Here we go - Il fait beau*

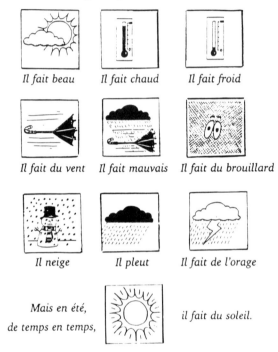

Il fait beau   Il fait chaud   Il fait froid

Il fait du vent   Il fait mauvais   Il fait du brouillard

Il neige   Il pleut   Il fait de l'orage

Mais en été,   il fait du soleil.
de temps en temps,

Using the OHP and individually cut out symbols for the weather expressions, each line can be briskly built up on a one, two, three basis;

e.g.   ONE - Each visual from the line is introduced and repeated by the class individually and then removed.

TWO - Then two visuals from the line are introduced and repeated in sequence.

THREE - Then the third visual is added to the line and the three visuals are repeated in sequence.

Before setting the visuals to the football tune, as many lines are built up in this way as possible. Some classes might only manage to recall six expressions and sing the tune by using just the first two lines, while others are quite capable of remembering all ten expressions, including the refinements of the last line.

You all sing the song! Then individual cut-outs can be removed to see if pupils can remember the missing expressions and so on. In the end, most pupils can sing the whole song from memory.

Well, if song works, why not try dance?

★   USING DANCE STEPS TO REINFORCE DIRECTIONS

With a group of pupils learning German in Year 8, problems were arising in following even the simplest directions on a straightforward grid (see figure 3). The difficulty for some pupils was in the concept of telling right from left in any language.

Figure 3   *Tango tanzen und singen - Wegbeschreibung*

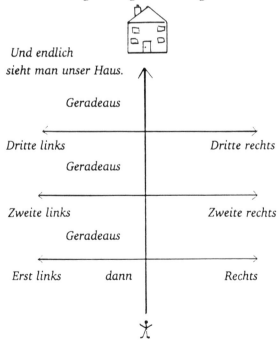

Und endlich sieht man unser Haus.

Geradeaus

Dritte links   *Dritte rechts*

Geradeaus

Zweite links   *Zweite rechts*

Geradeaus

Erst links   *dann*   *Rechts*

The German expressions and the visual support of the direction grid begged to be set to a tango rhythm set to the tune of *Fernando's hideaway*.

Pupils looked first to the left then to the right
- and moved forward in little steps.

Then they took two steps to the left and two to the right
- and moved forward in little steps.

Then three steps to the left and three to the right
- moving forward in little steps for the last time.

They took partners and, facing the same direction, repeated the song and dance. I cannot say that the footwork was anything like a professional tango, nor would it have scored highly on 'Come dancing', but it is remarkable how pace, rhythm, song and dance can refresh the parts that more traditional techniques fail to reach!

3   Use of the target language

So where does this leave us in relation to using the target language?

It is a popularly held view that the less able the learner the less feasible it becomes to use the target language for classroom management. This is a contentious issue, but I believe there are ways to promote the use of the target language which actively enhance the learning of the less able; techniques which include rather than exclude the learners and increase their motivation and independence from the teacher.

Setting an example

Start as we mean to go on! Pupils are far more willing to use the target language once they perceive it as natural. They are creatures of habit; if they are used to hearing the target language as the normal means of classroom communication from day one, they usually adapt to it and respond very readily. Hearing their teacher chatting to colleagues in French or German in the corridor and sharing a joke conveys strong messages about the language they are learning: foreign languages are real communication and French is not just the game they play from 9.00 until 10.00.

How do non-specialist teachers cope?

It is important where classes are shared that each teacher adopts similar approaches to classroom management and the use of the target language. If the teacher is a non-specialist, we have found it very helpful to make out a checklist of *phrases nécessaires*, so that non-specialist staff are equally as confident and supported as the pupils. This also ensures that the same language is being used by all staff to give instructions. This decreases the chance of pupils becoming confused.

It is also a good idea to draw up a list of expressions which praise and encourage pupils. The non-specialist teacher is then in a better position to maintain some form of constant communication in the target language beyond the defined input of a particular lesson.

Creating a secure environment

The key to ensuring a positive response to the target language is to provide a secure environment with plenty of support, so that the pupils never feel threatened or left out. If they do feel threatened, the resulting stress usually manifests itself in tears, sulks or disruptive behaviour.

It is essential with pupils with learning difficulties to be particularly sensitive to situations which could embarrass or humiliate pupils. In whole class presentations, where pupils are jumping up and down, miming, chanting or singing, some pupils prefer to sit it out and just watch. That is fine. They are learning in their own way, basking in the *bain linguistique*. They will join in when they are ready.

Pupil reaction

By sheer exposure to the target language, pupils soon pick up support phrases or instructions like:

> *Wie sagt man das auf Englisch? Du bist dran?*
> *C'est quoi en anglais? A toi le tour?*

They may still find the need to simultaneously translate and go through a phase of repeating everything in English just for the security of knowing that they have understood. There may then come a phase of 'inter-language', when they start making up their own rules: *Peux-tu pass me your règle, s'il te plaît?* This phase passes and the more exposure they have to the target language, the faster they transfer from receptive understanding to independent use.

Useful games

Explicit teaching of classroom language and instructions can also be of good value and great fun. Variations of *Simon dit*, *Give us a clue* and *Blockbusters* have all been successful in reinforcing the language required (see figure 4).

Figure 4 *Grille de 'Blockbusters'*

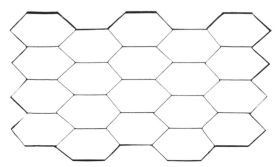

Exemplaire de vocabulaire et phrases utiles pour le jeu

J de C	-	Jeu de cartes	P?	-	Posez une question	O	-	Ordinateur
C de B	-	Cahier de brouillons	D	-	Dessinez	R	-	Règle
R	-	Regardez	T en G	-	Travaillez en groupes	C	-	Casque
Ch de P	-	Changez de place	R en O	-	Remettez en ordre	l	-	Logiciel
M	-	Magnétophone	AVLT	-	A vous le tour	S	-	Stylo
C la C	-	Cochez la case	G	-	Gomme	F	-	Feuille
E	-	Ecrivez	Ch	-	Chantez			

Naturally, it is asking too much of pupils with learning difficulties to sustain communication with each other in the target language throughout the entire lesson, including group work. There will be occasions when it is perfectly appropriate to revert to the mother tongue in order to make sense of their experiences. However, one class came up with a useful strategy to emphasise the use of the target language. They invented *Tirelire francophone* - a version of the *Swear box*.

For a defined part of the lesson, nobody uses anything other than the target language. If somebody speaks in English, they pay a fine of 1p. At the end of the term the money is used for a class party or prizes. The benefit of this is that the pupils control the *Tirelire* and discipline each other. The length of time that it operates can of course increase as progress is made in using the target language.

The foreign alphabet

Teaching the alphabet is a high priority on my list, because as soon as the written word is introduced, I like to enable the pupils to build words and to recognise and respond to the names of letters in the foreign alphabet. This puts them in a far stronger position with regard to pronunciation. For instance, getting those tongues in the right place for the French dental 'Ts' and 'Ds' early enough avoids words like *très* sounding like the chipped formica thing you find in the canteen. Later on in their learning, pupils can check on the accuracy of their spelling, while still remaining in the target language.

e.g. *Wie schreibt man das auf Deutsch?*
    Comment ça s'écrit en français?

This does not mean a dry academic approach to learning. Here are a couple of suggested activities which have been extremely popular.

★ THE ALPHABET CHANT

Pupils are divided into two teams and face each other. They then chant the alphabet like the American army on their morning jog; one side first and then the other.

ABCDEFG		VWXYZ		
	ABCDEFG		VWXYZ	
HIJKLMN		AB		CD
	HIJKLMN		AB		CD etc
OPQRSTU				
	OPQRSTU			

They can shake off their inhibitions and enjoy making sounds by varying the volume, speed or quality of the chant; sometimes trying to chant more loudly than the first team or sometimes more softly; faster or slower; like an opera singer; like a teenage Ninja mutant turtle, etc.

★ WORD CONSTRUCTION

Prepare a list of familiar words in which each letter of the alphabet appears only once. With the pupils still in two teams and with two sets of letter cards, pupils are given letters of the alphabet and become those letters. They physically respond to the spelling of a word by running to opposite ends of the classroom and forming that word. The first team with the correct version wins the point.

How can visuals promote the use of the target language, independence and group work?

The presentation techniques described earlier rely heavily on visuals and mime. The mime or 'action pictures' support the visuals and reduce the need for further explanation in English. The visuals then become the perfect stimulus for a variety of communicative activities in pairs and groups.

However, mixing your visuals can prove as big a headache as mixing your drinks! To illustrate the point, let us return to the earlier perils of the washing instructions label ...

If the circle with the cross through it means I can't put the baby's romper suit in the tumble drier, what does the circle inside the square with the cross through it mean???

We have already considered that visuals only work if everybody knows what they mean. What we now conclude is that visuals only work if we are consistent.

Developing a symbol convention

Once we have devised the visuals and involved our pupils in actively responding to them, we must make sure we stick to the same symbols throughout. We need to build up a symbol convention which introduces the language and can then be used to create the communicative games and tasks for subsequent phases of learning.

This may seem pure common sense, but how often are we guilty of exposing our least able pupils to an assortment of different visual clues: our drawings on the whiteboard, which may well vary from one lesson to the next; the text book; the worksheet; an excerpt from another text book; a photocopiable work card from, yes, yet another course book! Each time a new code to crack, another obstacle in their path. Each time another excuse to lose heart and have a chat in English. These are often the pupils with poor visual memory. We need to reinforce the images and words, not detract from them.

Self-help material based on a symbol convention

Developing a symbol convention simplifies learning and offers the pupils more flexibility in taking the learning away from the teacher. Providing self-help material based on the symbol convention can liberate pupils and allow them to learn at their own pace. Self-help sheets which include the symbols and the relevant language to be used in the communicative games and tasks are particularly effective in encouraging independence. So, too, are 'talking picture dictionaries'. This is really just a glorified name for self-help sheets of symbols and words accompanied by a tape. These are very useful for those pupils who need further consolidation of new material or who were absent when the input was given. All they need is the self-help sheet, the accompanying tape, a cassette recorder and a headset and they can then take charge of their own learning, playing and re-playing the tape as many times as they require. Once they are ready, they can then join in with group activities.

Visuals and the multi-activity classroom

Taking the topic of 'The weather' once again, we can see how the presentation involving visuals and 'action pictures' can lead to a range of communicative tasks. Figure 5 shows a few examples from a bank of communicative activities which make use of the same symbol convention and self-help material.

Figure 5 *Exemplaires d'activités qui utilisent les mêmes symboles*

1. Information gap Partenaire A   Partenaire B

2. Jeu de morpion (noughts and crosses)

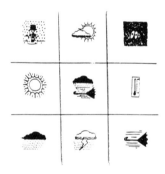

3. Concept keyboard overlay

1.	Effleurez les villes
2.	Découvrez la météo
3.	Mettez le symbole dessus

4. Partie de dominos

5. Listening grid

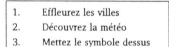

Cochez la case					
Paris					
Nice					
Clacton					
Londres					
Dieppe					

14

The class breaks into five groups of six. The intention is to provide some activities which do not require teacher intervention. This releases the teacher to support individual pupils or particular activities, for example the information-gap activity, where specialist help may be needed.

★ Activity 1   **Information-gap pair work**

- Partner A has an orange card showing the weather chart for five towns out of ten.
- Partner B has a lemon card showing the weather chart for the other five towns.
- By asking and answering questions, they swop information.

★ Activity 2   *'Jeu de morpion'/Noughts and crosses* **on the OHP**

- The group of six subdivides into threes.
- Using movable transparencies, the teams set and reset the game themselves.

★ Activity 3   **Concept keyboard pelmanism**

- A set of weather symbols on card are placed face down on the table.
- Each pupil takes it in turns to touch a town on the concept keyboard overlay and read the simple weather forecast displayed on the screen.
- They then turn over a symbol card.
- If it matches they place it on the town and win a point.
- The game continues until all cards are placed and the weather chart is completed.

★ Activity 4   *'Partie de Dominos'*

- A game of *picture dominoes*, matching the text to the symbols.

★ Activity 5   **Listening activity using junction box and headset**

- An activity involving ticking a grid to record a variety of weather conditions in different places in Europe, including their own town!

This is one example from a series of listening activities designed for pupils to use independently from the teacher. They are in charge of the tape and can listen to the French as often as they like. Instructions are given in French, but there is a limited amount of English back-up on the tape. No English is used on the task sheets. This is particularly beneficial for pupils with a below average reading age in the mother tongue, as it allows them to succeed in the activity by using just the visuals, the tape and their self-help sheets. Their inability in English does not impair their achievement in the foreign language.

The symbol convention introduced in the presentation phase gives continuity and makes all of the follow-up activities more accessible without constant recourse to English.

Building a resources bank

Gradually building up a resources bank of activities which employ the same symbols enables pupils to work alone or in pairs and groups without over-dependence on the teacher. The variety offered by adopting this kind of system cannot be emphasised enough (see figure 6).

This way of organising the learning implies a change in role for the teacher. We have to check ourselves from interfering when we are not invited. It is just as important not to offer help before it is needed as it is to recognise when assistance is required. By allowing pupils greater freedom to choose the activities which suit them best, pupils are genuinely involved in planning their own progress.

How do we keep English down to a minimum in setting up group work?

There can be a gap between the presentation phase and the multi-activity phase. As has been suggested, we can bridge the gap by adopting a symbol convention which offers the key to the language input. Explicit teaching of classroom instructions, like in the *Blockbusters* example, will also promote the use of the target language and better prepare the pupils to follow instructions as they move into pairs or groups.

However, certain group activities and games, which are simple and enjoyable to do, become impossibly complicated if you try to explain them by written instructions. If this is the case, there is no substitute for active demonstration in what is best described as a communicative warm up!

Figure 6   Designing a symbol convention

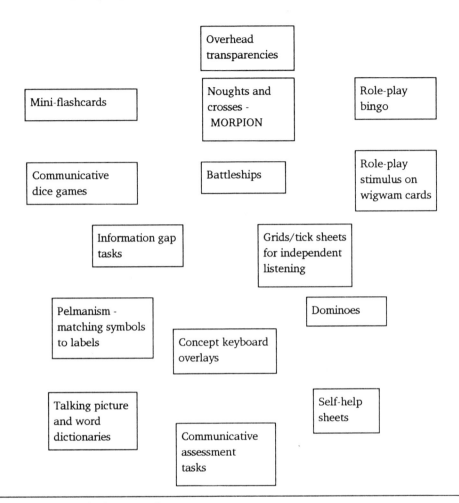

Designing a symbol convention

The benefits of designing a consistent symbol convention for the introduction of new language cannot be overemphasised. The symbols need to be simple, easily copiable by pupils and as unambiguous as possible. There is usually someone in the department who is a talented artist, or, if not, I have had pupils who have volunteered to draw up a set of symbols at home or in art and design lessons for use in class. The master copy should be in black and white line drawings, preferably on card. It can then be photocopied, cut and pasted for a variety of purposes.

4   Pre-communicative practice and support

Mind the gap

Before launching into communicative activities, pupils with learning difficulties need to practise language in a supported environment to a far greater extent than the more able learner. They will have to be involved in active demonstrations of how tasks and games work. If we are going to equip the learners for independence, this practice and support must be conducted in the target language. However, this intense level of exposure to the language can cause problems. We have to strike a careful balance between teacher-orchestrated activities and pupil involvement. The teacher must never be too dominant.

The intention of pre-communicative practice is gradually to reduce the reliance on the teacher and enable pupils to learn at their own pace. Pupils learn through what they do, not through what they are told.

So, pre-communicative practice should be equally as active as the presentation phase and, wherever possible, it should exploit the intrinsic motivations of the learners. What we are trying to achieve is to set the newly acquired language from the presentation phase in a communicative context which mirrors the tasks that are to follow.

Creating an information-gap

The concept of an information-gap for pupils with learning difficulties is sometimes hard to grasp, particularly if the course materials we use rely heavily on lengthy instructions in English. By the time the pupils have waded through the jocular scenario and have asked for further information from their friend or the teacher, the foreign language input required to complete the task seems very remote indeed and has often been completely erased.

Using the overhead projector and the pupils' creativity, albeit in a predetermined framework, information-gap activities can be created, demonstrated and rehearsed in a dynamic way, before we unleash pupils to attempt them on their own.

★   *WEGBESCHREIBUNG*

Using the direction grid (see figure 3 on p 7) and movable transparencies of different places around the town, the teacher can invite the class to design an area of the town.

Teacher asks: *Wie komme ich am besten zum Schloß, bitte?*
A suggestion is taken from the class: *Geradeaus*
Teacher places transparency in the appropriate place on the grid.

die Kirche   das Schloß

der Zoo   das Stadion

Once the pupils have grasped the question form, pupils come out and perform the task, building and rebuilding the town. The teacher's role becomes purely one of support, if things go wrong.

This activity can be reinforced later as A/B pair work, as part of a circus of different activities on 'Directions'. Each pupil has a grid and a set of the same place symbols on card. Pupil A designs his/her town. Pupil B asks questions about the directions to different places and responds to the information given by putting the appropriate picture on the relevant part of the map. Once pupil B has completed his/her grid, he/she can check against pupil A's master grid to see if everything is correct.

Movable symbols

Movable symbols are especially valuable for pupils with learning difficulties.

- They assist pupils with short-term memory by providing an instant and physical prompt.
- There is no need for recourse to English.
- Where motor skills are less developed, no anxiety is caused nor time wasted in drawing pictures to demonstrate comprehension.
- They create an open-ended dimension to what would have been a closed task, if the symbols had been predetermined and printed on the pair work cards.
- They provide a check-back facility for self-assessment.
- They are very flexible for use in other communicative games and activities, e.g. *Pelmanism, Snap, Happy Families* role-play, prompts for mixed-skill concept keyboard activities, and many more.

'Old friends are the best friends'

A great deal of mileage can be supplied by adapting familiar games to rehearse exchanges of information. Again, the advantage of using familiar games is the fact that laborious instructions in English can be avoided because the basic concepts and rules are already well known. A short demonstration from the teacher, reinforcing the foreign language elements from the presentation phase, is usually quite adequate and pupils can easily take the pace of the learning away from the teacher and run the game themselves for as long or as short a time as they require. Here are a couple of personal favourites.

★ *NOUGHTS AND CROSSES* AS PREPARATION FOR A CLASS SURVEY - YEAR 9

Once again the overhead projector and movable transparencies come into their own. As preparation for a *Sondage* on 'Weekend activities', the class divides into two teams. Following one round organised by the teacher, pupils volunteer to run the game themselves. Two pupils, one from each team, are needed at the OHP.

The whole game practises the question form: *Qu'est-ce que tu fais le weekend?* and up to a dozen answer forms, e.g. *je fais du lèche-vitrine, je joue au football, je vais à la disco,* etc.

The game is set by a *remue-méninges* around the class, i.e. the question is put and the class 'brainstorms' different suggestions from the initial input. The visuals are adjacent to the OHP and the pupils pick out the correct symbols and build up the *Noughts and crosses* board. The images should be projected onto a whiteboard not a screen, so that the noughts and crosses can be marked up using a dry marker pen and easily erased to allow for the game to be played and reset easily.

The game is then played by pupil A asking a member of his/her team:
   Qu'est-ce que tu fais le weekend?

Once the answer is given, pupil A marks a nought on the whiteboard.

If pupil A cannot recognise what his/her team member has answered, pupil B has the opportunity to claim the space for the 'Crosses' team. Then it becomes pupil B's turn and so the game goes on.

★   ROLE-PLAY *BINGO* - YEAR 9

A communicative A/B grid activity on 'Making a date', *La vie en rose*, places quite considerable demands on the memory for pupils with learning difficulties (see figure 7). As we know only too well, there comes a limit to the amount of listening, demonstration and repetition that these learners can stomach before the need to be actively involved. Active involvement with discrete, well-packaged topics is easy and fun to organise, but preparing pupils with learning difficulties adequately for a dialogue of this complexity can be a headache. If we overexpose them to the image of the grid itself, they will rapidly become disenchanted with it, without even beginning to use it communicatively.
   Role-play *Bingo* has proved a winner with many Year 9 pupils. It gives them the opportunity to listen **actively** to the necessary language and familiarise themselves with it painlessly.
   Using the same symbol convention that has been consistent throughout their learning, the pupils design their own *Bingo* card, following a short demonstration on the OHP by the teacher (see figure 8).

Figure 7   *Rendez-vous - La vie en rose*

Personne	Lieu	Quand ça?	A quelle heure?	Lieu de rendez-vous

Explication d'activité
Partenaire A invite partenaire B à sortir.
Tous les deux notent les détails de rendez-vous.
Plus tard, on vérifie les détails.

Dialogue
A: *Comment t'appelles-tu?*

B: *Shelley. Et toi?*

A: *Daniel.*
Si on allait au concert?

B: *Je veux bien! Quand ça?*

A: *Jeudi soir*

B: *A quelle heure?*

A: *A vingt heures trente*

B: *On se revoit où?*

A: *Devant le théâtre?*

B: *D'accord!*

Figure 8   Role-play *bingo* card

They select:
- three possible places to go
  (from a choice of ten);
- three possible days of the week;
- three possible times to meet
  (from a choice of ten);
- three possible places to meet
  (from a choice of ten).

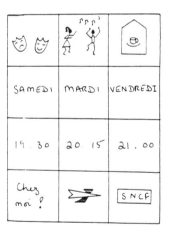

The teacher goes through the dialogue in sequence, picking up symbol cards and offering two or three alternatives per line, e.g.:

Si on allait **au ciné**? *Si on allait* **au match de foot**?
Je veux bien!
Quand ca? - **Lundi**? - **Vendredi**? - **Dimanche**?
D'accord?
A quelle heure? **12.00**, **16.00**, **19.30**?
On se revoit où? **Chez toi**? **A la gare**? **Au café**?
The first pupil to have crossed a symbol in each line, thus making a complete date, shouts out *Rendez-vous!* and wins the game.

Pre-communicative support can be conducted with the whole class or with smaller groups within a mixed-ability framework.

Variety in role-play preparation for less able learners in mixed-ability classes

As many different stimuli as possible are required to 're-activate' and revitalise topics from the very start of the learning programme. In lockstep approaches, reliant on a limited number of tasks from the standard text book, small groups of less able learners in mixed-ability classes can be left behind and never catch up if they fail to meet with instant success at the same time as everyone else. They may well be capable of achieving the same objectives as others in the class, but will require fresh and more frequent opportunities to prepare and demonstrate their achievement.

We can lose learners from as early as the first term if we throw them into more open-ended communicative activities too soon, so that they experience failure. Equally, we can go into overkill with 'safe', over-rehearsed class practice.

The topic of 'Personal information' is riddled with pitfalls. You know you are in deep trouble when you hear yourself saying: *John, John! Wie heißt du, John?* No wonder he looks puzzled!

We need as many new ways as possible to offer imaginative opportunities to use and re-use the necessary language for this topic. Here are some examples.

★ *WIGWAM* CARDS

Wigwam cards with a symbol convention for the questions on one side and imaginary and often wildly eccentric characters invented by other pupils on the other are all good value (see figure 9).

Figure 9   Example of a *Wigwam* Card

★ COMMUNICATIVE DICE GAMES

Communicative games which rely on the luck of the dice and exchanges of information in order to win can also provide a refreshing alternative (see figure 10).

Here we see a game for four players.

There are six categories:
Prénom, Age, Ville, Animal, Passetemps, Frères/Soeurs.

Each player has six coloured counters.

The winner is the first player to have placed a counter in each of the six categories.

Rules of the game:

Player A throws the dice.
If 3 is showing, player A must ask player B the question for Category 3:
    Ville: *Où habites-tu?*

In order to place the counter, player A must show that he/she has understood the reply, e.g.   *J'habite Nice*

Figure 10   Communicative dice game

PRENOM	SABINE	PIERRE	HELENE	MARC
AGE	14	12	13	11
VILLE	PARIS	LYON	AMIENS	NICE
ANIMAL				
PASSE-TEMPS				
FRERES/SOEURS				

Player A places counter on the square for Nice.
It is now player B's turn.

The answers are not prescriptive in the sense that any of the alternatives in each category can be given; the columns are not intended to be fixed 'personae'.

Each player only needs to place one counter on each category, so if player A threw a 3 again, he/she would simply forfeit a turn.

In this particular example 24 exchanges of information are possible. This is already quite challenging for pupils with learning difficulties. The more capable they become, however, the more exchanges of information are possible. With a ten-sided dice up to 100 exchanges of information can be made. The mere fact that this is a game provides an incentive to play again and again and a communicative context in which to rehearse particular exchanges of information before conducting a more open-ended 'personal conversation'.

Follow-up assignments for older pupils

A popular follow-up assignment has been to invite the pupils to make up their own answer board for other pupils, comprising as many categories and alternatives as they can recall. A self-help sheet (prepared on the word processor, if available) and/or reference tape in the target language accompanies the game to help other players. Rather than drawings, pictures from magazines have been used. In this way older pupils have no objection to playing the game, because it does not look infantile.

Time and money are always of the essence. Therefore, the more uses that can be obtained from one set of visuals the better. With a very low ability group learning *Des fruits au marché,* a set of cards for *Pelmanism* - pictures of fruits mounted on pale blue card and labels for the fruits mounted on apricot coloured card, has proved very versatile.

The cards are all placed face down on the table. The game is suitable for a group of up to six players. The idea is to turn over two cards, one blue, one apricot, and try to match up the pictures to the labels. Trying to recall the position of the cards stimulates the memory and assists in reinforcing recognition of the written word.

The same cards can be used for a rehearsal of role-play in the form of a version of *Happy Families.* The idea is to pair up the label to the picture. In order to do so, players carry out the following transactional dialogue:

> *Vous avez des pêches, Madame?*
> If yes, the reponse is: *Oui, combien en voulez-vous?*
> *Un kilo, s'il vous plâit! Ça fait combien?*
> *F.32.00, Madame!*   (Looking at the price tag on the picture.)
> *Merci, au revoir!*   (Pupil takes the picture card and wins a point for placing the pair.)

If the player asked does not have the picture, the answer *Désolée, il n'y en a plus!* is given and it becomes the next player's turn.

The game may only be a rehearsal, but it is nevertheless constructed on communicative principles and promotes mixed-skill development: a question prompted by reading a label is asked; understanding is demonstrated by supplying a visual clue; a check-back is provided by matching the visual to the label.

So, to re-cap. Pre-communicative support can involve the whole class or purely a selected group within a mixed-ability class. There is a careful balance between the teacher demonstrating how tasks and activities work and pupil involvement in the demonstration. In a game, once the rules are known, the pupils can manage the activity for as long or as short a time as they require, as a prelude to further communicative tasks. These might range from a survey or an interview grid involving the whole class to an information-gap activity or a board or card game conducted in pairs or small groups as part of a circus of other activities. To define the jargon as I use it, 'pre-communicative' describes the phase of learning rather than the activities used within that phase. The activities in themselves will always be based on communicative principles and rely on the exchange of information.

5   Organising the multi-activity classroom

Following pre-communicative practice, pupils with learning difficulties benefit from a range of opportunities to continue learning at their own pace and demonstrate what they already know and can do. Developing independence and offering variety and choice puts different demands on classroom organisation, management and use of resources. However, with the bare minimum of equipment much can be achieved.

The essentials are:
- an overhead projector
- at least two small cassette recorders
- two junction boxes and headsets
- a free-standing computer
- a concept keyboard - often this can be shared with the SEN department
- sturdy but light-weight tables and chairs that can be stacked easily to free floor space or moved to facilitate group work
- a room with a carpet and black-out facilities
- access to a television and video
- plenty of power points at strategic places in the room.

A circus of communicative activities

In the shift in emphasis from whole class activities to more independent learning, many teachers opt firstly for a controlled environment, where a core of four or five activities are available and all groups eventually complete the tasks during a given lesson or series of lessons, e.g.

- information-gap activities - supported by the teacher if necessary;
- independent listening using a junction box and headsets;
- investigative reading - using self-help sheets if required;
- mixed-skill activities around the concept keyboard;
- a communicative board or card game.

In this model, management difficulties are largely overcome by providing self-help material and answer cards. Pupils are encouraged to control the equipment themselves and this benefits the learning process.

Pupil autonomy and individual routes

A more ambitious model is to allow pupils much more flexibility in choosing their own routes through a range of possibilities offering assignments at different levels of complexity and challenge. Pupils should never be forced into activities which extend them beyond their capabilities, but neither should their expectations be kept artificially low by denying them the chance to try their hand at more difficult tasks, if they want to. With some guidance from the teacher, they should select those activities best suited to their needs and interests.

Particularly in Key Stage 4, this model is most effective because it places much more responsibility on the learner and reduces the possibility of conflict, which can arise in more teacher-dominated situations. Pupils become much more involved in planning their own progress and keeping a record or diary of what they have done, how well they did it and what they felt about it. By providing sample sentences and making simple substitutions to build up different meanings, these records of achievement can be kept in the foreign language.

This more autonomous model does not imply the disappearance of whole class activities and pre-communicative support. Active presentation techniques and teacher-orchestrated activities maintain their place, but a healthy balance must exist between the 'all singing, all dancing' stimulus and the individual opportunities to internalise and experiment, apply, re-apply and extend the language acquired.

Tips for designing or choosing suitable course materials

- It is best to have as little text as possible on a page.

- Avoid extended instructions - once a sentence runs over more than one line, it becomes more difficult to grasp.

- Keep to simple instructions in the target language supported by visual clues. Only offer crib sheets in English as the final resort.

- Keep recorded instructions in English to a minimum.

- Opt for answer grids or tick charts which are easy to use and do not rely on intricate explanation.

- Choose a round, open type face or clear rounded handwriting with easily definable upstrokes and downstrokes. Try to keep consistent with the typeface you use.

- When photocopying reading material, choose pastel backgrounds, preferably yellows, apricots and pinks. Evidence has shown that the combination of black print on white is the most unsuitable for slow readers.

- Look for materials which use a consistent symbol convention.

- Opt for courses which offer variety in stimulus material and plenty of self-access reinforcement activities at different levels of difficulty.

- Investigate the possibility of buying a licence from your publisher which allows you to 'customise' taped material for your pupils' needs.

- Try to find published material which seems to be written about and designed for teenagers and does not look like a text book.

General hints in designing reading cards or recording listening material

- Always start and end with something easy.
  Nothing is more motivating than success.

- In more demanding tasks, try, if possible, to include some personal element like the name of a pupil, teacher or foreign language assistant(e), street in the town, name of a youth club, etc. This never fails to grab their attention. Curiosity and thirst for scandal arouse their desire to find out more!

6   Maintaining motivation in Key Stage 4

There seems to be a strange tendency to cut down on pupils' physical activity and freedom to move about the classroom in direct proportion to their physical size - the bigger they get, the greater the temptation to take out the super glue and fix them to their seats! This creates immense problems. The less we feel we can trust the learners, the more they will live up to our lack of confidence.

If we can get the 'recipes' right during the first three years of language learning, then the pupils we take through into Key Stage 4 will begin with a very healthy self-image. We need to foster their independence and build on the positive foundations of:

- active involvement;
- starting from the learners' own experiences;
- variety of stimulus;
- a secure environment;
- pupil choice.

We must ensure that they have equal opportunities to be involved in more ambitious assignments. This does not imply more complex language or less support but a wider variety of contexts for learning; increased access to real 'audiences'; greater possibilities in linking with other subject areas in setting up specific projects; chances to take their learning outside the confines of the classroom.

Real tasks for real purposes

For pupils with learning difficulties, the way they learn, 'the process' is naturally of special importance, but the outcome, 'the product' perhaps assumes an even greater significance than is the case with more able learners. They need to be reassured that the activities they engage in are valid in themselves and have tangible results. They need to see the fruits of their labours.

★ SURVEYS AND RELEVANCE

We can trust pupils with learning difficulties to move around and conduct surveys, if they fully understand why they are doing it and what they are going to do with the information they discover. The value of the activity must not purely be to rehearse particular language components, otherwise, to the pupils' way of thinking, it is pointless. They should be offered the opportunity to use the information in a positive way; displaying their findings in pie charts and bar graphs. There is nothing new in cashing in on their principle pre-occupation, 'watching TV', but how about involving them in conducting a survey across other classes in their year group or with older students studying 'A' level! They can then make comparisons between TV viewing habits in their class with those of other classes and draw simple conclusions. Perhaps the findings could be displayed, using desk top publishing and presented in some bi-lingual magazine for the school's Euro Week. The language may be simple but the task seems relevant and mature.

Instead of rehearsing 'Means of transport' - *Comment est-ce que tu viens à l'école?* just for the sake of it, add a 'green' element to it; how many people travel by car; how many use *de l'essence sans plomb* and how many *de l'essence plombifère.* Using the springboard of the survey, a bilingual poster campaign can be mounted in collaboration with the science department to promote 'green awareness' - *choisissez le vert!* for the Europe of the '90s. The kudos in this kind of project really maintains motivation and raises morale.

★ PROVIDING AN AUDIENCE

There may be a number of sensitive issues which preclude certain pupils with learning difficulties from participation in house-to-house exchange visits. However, contacts with real French people and real German people, even if it is only through exchange tapes and materials, give substance to the learning and provide an 'audience' and a reason for communicating and producing brochures, videos, photo-montage, tapes, etc. Any possibility of drafting in visiting foreign nationals should not be wasted and if and when they do come into school, we should try to ensure that projects involving pupils with learning difficulties are included in the planning, e.g.

a. A very successful assignment in one lower ability group was to make a photo-montage accompanied by a tape of *Une journée dans la vie au collège* to show to groups of visiting French students, staying at a local summer school.

b. Another success was a guided tour on video accompanied by a brochure of a residential Special School. It was made entirely in German by a group of fifteen-year-old boys with emotional and behavioural difficulties, in preparation for the return visit of their German exchange partners, who are also in Residential Education. Valuable cross-curricular links were made with Media Studies. The boys made a professional attempt at designing a story-board for their video in English and German, acquired editing skills and 'voice-over' techniques, *Auf Deutsch, natürlich!*

★ JIGSAW READING AND LISTENING FROM REAL MATERIAL

Pupils with learning difficulties rarely maintain penfriend communication in the traditional sense, but considerable benefits can be derived from setting up class links in the form of tape and 'dossiers' exchanges. Producing and swopping 'dossiers' and tapes from one class to another can supply a wealth of real material. Much of the material is suitable for jigsaw reading and listening activities.

Figure 11   Jigsaw listening and reading

Salut! C'est moi, Bénédicte!
Aujourd'hui c'est le neuf avril.
C'est mon anniversaire!
Je fête mes quinze ans.

Ici à la maison, nous sommes cinq.
Ma mère, ma grand-mère, mes frères,
et moi.

J'aime beaucoup le collège.
Mes profs sont sympas.
Surtout j'adore le prof de géo.
Il est jeune et amusant.

Je suis très sportive.
Je fais beaucoup de sport au
collège et pendant les vacances.
Le patin à roulettes, c'est chouette!

Nom:	Anniversaire:	Age:

Famille:		Collège:

Loisirs:	Où?	Quand?

Pupils gather information and classify it on a grid by first listening to the tape and noting down what they can and then by reading the relevant 'dossier' and adding to their existing discoveries (see figure 11). The classes and teachers need to agree the particular themes for each 'dossier' and tape exchange in advance. The class involvement in choosing the themes is essential if they are going to be interested in finding out what is in the package, when it arrives.

There are two essential differences and advantages which distinguish this scheme from the traditional 'penfriend' system:

a. The onus of sustaining communication does not have to fall on one individual: 'Neville's' gang of friends makes a tape and puts a 'dossier' together for 'Jean-Loup's' gang of friends and vice versa.

b. The pupils make the tapes and the 'dossiers' partly in French and partly in English. The French part of the assignment is completed in the language lessons and the English part is either done at home or is produced in co-operation with the English or Personal and Social Education departments.

Doing and making

Making something either for themselves, another class, an agency in the town, members of the family or their teachers can be very motivating, e.g.

★ *HIMMEL UND HÖLLE SPIEL* (see figure 12).

A paper game made by following German instructions, assisted by diagrams and then used as a novel stimulus for role-play. *Wegbeschreibung* is only one example. Many different topics could be used either by the maker or by another class.

★ MAKING A CONCEPT KEYBOARD OVERLAY FOR ANOTHER CLASS

A good example was a game called *Fundbüro*, where pupils made up the overlay of different pictures of personal items like a pair of gloves, a key-ring, a jacket, a handbag, gym shoes, etc in black and white line drawings. They also produced a pack of mini-flashcards of the same personal items in a range of colours, e.g. a blue pair of gloves, a red pair, yellow pair, green pair, etc. The players each pick up a mini-flashcard.

Pupil A operating the board asks: *Was haben Sie verloren?*

Pupil B gives the answer according to the picture card: *Ich habe meine Jacke verloren.*

Pupil A finds and touches the picture of the jacket and the message on the screen says, e.g.: *Man hat eine grüne Jacke gefunden.*

Figure 12   *Himmel und Hölle*

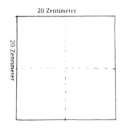

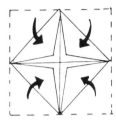

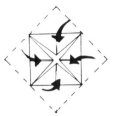

1. *Das Blatt entlang der gestrichelten Linien falten!*

2. *Die Rückseite nach oben drehen und die Ecken zur Mitte umklappen!*

3. *Das gefaltete Blatt umdrehen und die Ecken wieder zur Mitte umklappen!*

4. *Die Mitte eindrücken! Man kann jetzt die Figur beschriften.*

Außen - die Zahlen
Innen   - Symbole für die Ortsangaben
Unten - Symbole für die Wegbeschreibung

5. *Zum Spielbeginn die Finger beider Hände in die Höhlen stecken und die vier Ecken so zusammenschließen, daß nur die Zahlen sichtbar sind.*

Spielverlauf

A: *Eins, zwei, drei usw.*

B: *Entschuldigung!*
     Wie komme ich am besten zum Bahnhof?

A: *Sie nehmen die erste Straße links und dann geradeaus.*
B: *Erste Straße links und dann geradeaus. Vielen Dank.*

A: *Nichts zu danken.*
     Auf Wiedersehen!
B: *Auf Wiedersehen!*

Das Spiel kann immer wieder von neuem gespielt werden, bis die Wegangaben nach allen Orten erfragt worden sind.

Die Schüler können die Rollen tauschen, so daß jeder einmal fragt und einmal antwortet.

He/she asks: *Welche Farbe hat Ihre Jacke?*

Pupil B answers according to the colour on the card: *Meine Jacke ist dunkelblau.*

Pupil A responds: *Es tut mir leid. Ihre Jacke ist nicht hier.*

Pupil B has to throw away that card by putting it back on the table face down and picks up another card. It then becomes the next player's turn.

32

If the personal item is the same colour on the mini-flashcard as on the screen message the player keeps the card, wins a point and has another turn.

The winner is the player with the most cards at the end of the game.

Simple but fun! Made by pupils for pupils! Making a self-help overlay to assist with the model dialogue and involving the foreign language assistant in helping with the *Spielregeln* provide further meaningful activities.

★ TURNING A CONCEPT KEYBOARD OVERLAY INTO A VERSION OF A VIEW DATA SCREEN TO BE DISPLAYED IN THE LOCAL TOURIST OFFICE

Taking the theme of 'Leisure facilities', a simple map of the town with symbols marking the sites of the cinema, the swimming pool, the discos, the sports stadium, etc forms the master overlay. The pupils programme in different layers of information for the French tourist:

Level one: *La légende* - the relevant labels for the amenities.
Level two: The name, address and telephone number.
Level three: Opening hours.
Level four: Prices and group reductions.
Level five: Special details or What's On.
Level six: Details of refreshment facilities on site or nearby.

★ BLUE PETER *A LA FRANÇAISE*

Making a kite for a younger brother or sister from a template in French, involving measuring and cutting out according to metric measurements.

★ DESIGNING AND PRODUCING AN INVITATION

Using a desk top publishing package, pupils design an invitation to a *Déjeuner sur l'herbe* for the staff.

★ PREPARING A *DÉJEUNER SUR L'HERBE*

Linking with the Home Economics department and working through French, preparing the food for the lunch, including physically weighing and measuring ingredients using grammes and kilogrammes.

★ PHOTO MONTAGE

Taking photos of the lunch for follow-up display and caption writing. An additional activity can be provided by presenting the photos and captions in random order to another group and inviting them to mount them in the correct order and in so doing enabling them to develop their sequencing skills.

Expressing opinions

All too often it is assumed that pupils with learning difficulties have no opinions or that it is inappropriate and too complicated to expect them to express their views. Every pupil has a unique contribution to make and should have the opportunity to express personal points of view.

From the outset, pupils should be encouraged to evaluate even at a very simple level. By pinning up two large sheets of sugar paper on the display board, one entitled *'Ce que j'aime'* and the other *'Ce que je n'aime pas'*, pupils can begin to express feelings by adding items in writing or pasting up and labelling pictures cut out from magazines. A third section can be added, *'Pourquoi?'* and straightforward reasons can be included to justify the opinions expressed.

Making comparisons

★ CREATING A DATABASE

In addition to *Sondages,* designing and building a simple database has proved very popular even with pupils experiencing quite considerable learning difficulties. A particular favourite has been a 'dating agency', where the pupils enter their information under a pseudonym. The resulting *rencontres* when the identities are revealed can be hilarious.

The pupils decide on the 'fields' to be included, work out the questions they need to ask, interview each other, check that the information is correct, update information, search the database and compare fields. An added bonus in creating a database is that the part of the programme which requests you to explain the 'fields' actually provides excellent self-help material for pupils who have forgotten the necessary questions and answers.

★ USING THE MAIL ORDER CATALOGUE AS A MATURE PICTURE DICTIONARY

Independent learning can put the teacher in a very awkward position if the pupil asks for the appropriate French for some technical gadget that the teacher has never heard of! The mail order catalogue is a superb reference book, which the pupils thoroughly enjoy using without the teacher's intervention.

Catalogue 3 Suisses as a stimulus for communicative activities

We may blanch at the thought of using something like sections of a mail order catalogue as stimulus material for pupils with learning difficulties, due to the size of the script, and feel it necessary to 'authenticate' certain pages by producing word processed versions of the catalogue entries in a larger, more accessible form.

This may indeed be advisable for some of our learners as a preparation for the 'real thing'. However, it is my feeling that by Key Stage 4 we may well be doing our pupils a disservice if we do not expose them to 'real life' challenges and provide opportunities to develop transferable skills like cross-referencing, classifying choices and making decisions using authentic source materials. Tasks using *Catalogue 3 Suisses* provide such opportunities in a context already very familiar to many of the learners, who very probably have mail order catalogues at home. Here are a few examples of the sort of activities which pupils have enjoyed.

- Making comparisons between the range of consumer goods, the style, the price, etc offered by the French catalogue as opposed to the English one.

- Collaborative problem-solving, where the group is given a master card presenting the problem, e.g. ordering wedding presents, selecting an appropriate outfit for a person with weight problems, choosing a suitable pair of bedroom curtains, etc. Each member of the group has a card with a simple clue on it which he/she shares with the other members of the group in order to narrow down the choice and solve the problem. This means that no pupil has to read extended text, but they all have an equal contribution to make in finding the solution. As the clues or 'constraints' are shared around the group, they do not serve to complicate the task but simplify it and give it a structure.

- Using cut up magazines and the language of the catalogue as a model, the pupils make 'mock-ups' of their own mail order catalogue pages; each group taking a different range of products or goods.

- Bringing in items of their own clothing and once again adapting the language of the catalogue, they create their own mail order database, *Vêtements d'occasion*.

- Using the internal phonelines and the foreign language assistant(e), or as a 'back to back' pair work activity, they simulate 'placing an order by telephone' and filling in the details on a pro-forma.

Why do these activities succeed in motivating pupils with learning difficulties?

- The level of language necessary in these activities is quite simple; straightforward questions and answers, lists, labels, short phrases, advertising slogans, forms.

- There is always plenty of visual back-up.

- The context is familiar to most of the learners.

- The activities seem mature, sophisticated and relevant.

- The pupils are always actively involved. The learning is something they do, not something that is done to them.

7   Dismissing the 'can't do' agenda

For many colleagues, entitlement to foreign language learning for all abilities is not new. We have learnt much from development work in graded assessment and cross-curricular modular schemes like B. Tech with clearly defined goals.

Nonetheless, implementing the National Curriculum will undoubtedly present us with challenges, and challenge is never a bad thing. I hope that *Communication re-activated* has reviewed some of the relevant aspects of current good practice which will be the most appropriate in meeting the needs of pupils with learning difficulties and has provided some guidance on where to start in enhancing our existing provision.

We need to dispel from our minds the notion of what pupils 'can't do' and replace it with a positive agenda of what they can do and are currently doing in many classes up and down the country.

Fair access to resources, technical equipment and the support of foreign language assistant(e)s will certainly help us to provide a suitable learning environment for pupils experiencing learning difficulties. However, the love of language and the enjoyment of learning are engendered by our own attitudes towards the learners. If we believe in the value of 'languages for all', this will be transmitted to our pupils. There is no substitute for teacher enthusiasm.

The techniques and activities included in this book have been through the 'quality control' of the classroom. Not all tasks or methods are appropriate for all learners. It is best to 'pick and mix' and develop our own styles, involving the learners and taking them with us as we plan our programmes of study.

A final note from the pupils! Over the last year, on several occasions in different schools, pupils who were previously disenchanted with learning a foreign language have changed their views and have turned around and said:

'French is wicked!'

Well, that is good enough for me!